A Walk Thru the Life of

JOSEPH

The Power of Forgiveness

Walk Thru the Bible

BakerBooks

a division of Baker Publishing Group
Grand Rapids, Michigan

© 2009 by Walk Thru the Bible

Published by Baker Books
a division of Baker Publishing Group
P.O. Box 6287, Grand Rapids, MI 49516-6287
www.bakerbooks.com

Printed in the United States of America

Library of Congress Cataloging-in-Publication Data
A walk thru the life of Joseph : the power of forgiveness / Walk Thru the Bible.
   p. cm.
   Includes bibliographical references.
   ISBN 978-0-8010-7168-3 (pbk.)
   1. Joseph (Son of Jacob) 2. Bible. O.T. Genesis—Study and teaching. 3. Bible. O.T. Genesis—Criticism, interpretation, etc. I. Walk Thru the Bible (Educational ministry).
   BS580.J6W34 2009
   222′.11092—dc22   2008050831

Cover image: Kamchatka / iStock

Contents

3

Introduction

If you paid much attention to the public conversation in the media after Sept. 11, 2001, you heard a persistent theological question underneath it all: "Where was God when this happened?" For some people, that was just a nagging thought; others, however, voiced it plainly. The devastation that occurred, the number of lives that were mercilessly lost, and the damage it did to the psyche of the United States all raised the question of how such a catastrophe could occur under the watchful eye of the one so many of us call "Father." It just didn't make any sense.

That question comes up frequently in our personal lives too. Where is God when a friend is suffering from repeated physical abuse, or when our business goes bankrupt from a dishonest deal, or when a drunk driver causes the permanent paralysis of someone who definitely doesn't deserve it? Why doesn't God stand in the way of evil?

The answer is elusive. Our minds are filled with "what ifs" and "what nows" when the actions of human beings contradict the character of God. "What if so-and-so hadn't ruined my life?" "What did God have in store for me that I've missed?" "How many times can I blow it before God gives up on his 'perfect' will for my life?" We just don't know how to reconcile the chaos of a fallen world with his providence, and deep down, all of us wonder if it's too late. We've heard that God loves us and has wonderful plans for our lives, but if human error and sinful hearts mess up the will of God, where does life go from there? In other words, if someone has forfeited God's plan A, what's his plan B? Does he even have one?

Our angst over the capricious nature of life in a fallen world frequently turns to blame. We blame ourselves for the fine mess we got ourselves into, we blame others for the unfairness we suffer, and we blame God because he certainly could have prevented that unfairness if he wanted to. So obviously, he didn't want to. And for that, all of our existential complaints rise to the surface and linger unanswered. Why? Because we can't reconcile a sovereign God with our brutal twists of fate. We've heard that he works all things together for the good of those who love him, but not all things are good. Some things are downright disastrous. And when the mess is really overwhelming, the promised goodness seems really abstract. And distant. And very, very unlikely.

No one but God knows how often those questions arose in Joseph's heart as years and years passed by between his initial calling and its strange fulfillment. Joseph survived one of the world's most dysfunctional families, several years in a foreign prison, and a land and culture far removed from God's promises to his family. It had to be confusing. But Genesis nowhere hints that Joseph might have faltered in his faith. God's favor was with him throughout his life.

Joseph and His Family

Genesis begins to narrow its focus to a single family in chapter 12 with the call of Abraham and God's promise to make his descendants into a great nation that would bless the entire earth. Abraham's long-awaited son was named Isaac, who in turn had two sons named Jacob and Esau. God chose Jacob as the son through whom he would fulfill his covenant and changed his name to Israel. Joseph was the second youngest of Jacob's twelve sons. And though Abraham, Isaac, and Jacob are given substantial attention in Genesis, it becomes Joseph's story in chapters 37–50—over a fourth of the Bible's first book. Except for an interlude in chapter 38, Joseph's life is described in continuous narrative through the end of Genesis.

Because Jacob's two wives, Leah and Rachel, engaged in competitive childbearing (Genesis 30), Jacob had twelve sons and an unspecified number of daughters. Leah, the unloved wife, gave birth to six of those sons, and her maid gave birth to two of them. The loved wife, Rachel, was long barren and gave her maid to Jacob, who fathered two sons through her. Finally, Rachel bore a son of her own—Joseph—the firstborn of Jacob's one true love. And Rachel's second son caused her death in childbirth.

For that reason, Joseph was most highly favored by Jacob— which means he was most highly resented by the rest of the family. ("Favorite child" status remains a painful burden to bear in families today, both for the favorite and the siblings.) That may explain why his oldest brothers assigned him as assistant to the concubines' sons in the family work (Gen. 37:2); they felt a need to put him down. And that snub may explain why Joseph reported the bad behavior of the concubines' sons and why he felt it important to share his lofty dreams with the family; he felt a need to lift himself up. Regardless, these were complicated and volatile dynamics. Twelve sons from four different mothers living with a heartbroken father whose last fond memory of his favorite wife is her first son—that's enough to keep a busload of counselors in business.

Major Themes

God's sovereignty is one of the most prominent themes in the life of Joseph. How exactly does God's will intersect with human flaws? The Bible doesn't give us the details of the nature of God's sovereignty, but it is emphatic about the fact that God oversees everything and works his good intentions into every circumstance in which his people have faith in him (and even many in which they don't). But while many people see Genesis 50:20—"You intended to harm me, but God intended it for good to accomplish what is now being done"—as a foundational theological statement and the primary message of the story, there are so many subplots and symbolic elements that the narrative can be mined for insights for years. For example:

- The events of Joseph's life foreshadow the role and ministry of Jesus in remarkable detail.
- The pictures of redemption, forgiveness, and reconciliation are profound case studies in the character of God and, ideally, of his people.
- The message of how God provided for his people far in advance of their need is an inspiration and encouragement to our faith and prayers.
- The favor of God on Joseph's life speaks volumes about what it means to be called by God for a specific purpose.
- Joseph's management of the widespread regional famine dramatically demonstrates God's desire for his people to reach the nations and influence cultures with his mercy.
- The minority status of Hebrews in Egypt hints that the citizenship of the people of God rests in him alone and not in any location, language, or culture.

There's a wealth of information and wisdom in the life of Joseph that can be applied to our purpose in life, our relationship with God, our relationships with others, our financial steward-ship, our attitudes toward work, and the suffering we go through. Joseph lived a difficult life that was ultimately worth the grief—an illustration of a promise that we can apply to our own lives too. He found God to be faithful in every trial and discovered that in the kingdom of God, the glory of the destination always outweighs the pain of the journey to get there.

How to Use This Guide

The questions in this guide are geared to elicit every participant's input, regardless of his or her level of preparation. Obviously, the more group members prepare by reading the biblical text and the background information in the study guide, the more they will get out of it. But even in busy weeks that afford no preparation time, everyone will be able to participate in a meaningful way.

The discussion questions also allow your group quite a bit of latitude. Some groups prefer to briefly discuss the questions in order to cover as many as possible, while others focus only on one or two of them in order to have more in-depth conversations. Since this study is designed for flexibility, feel free to adapt it according to the personality and needs of your group.

Each session ends with a hypothetical situation that relates to the passage of the week. Discussion questions are provided, but group members may also want to consider role-playing the scenario or setting up a two-team debate over one or two of the questions. These exercises often cultivate insights that wouldn't come out of a typical discussion.

Regardless of how you use this material, the biblical text will always be the ultimate authority. Your discussions may take you to many places and cover many issues, but they will have the greatest impact when they begin and end with God's Word itself. And never forget that the Spirit who inspired the Word is in on the discussion too. May he guide it—and you—wherever he wishes.

A Family Fiasco

GENESIS 37

Identity is a complicated thing. Our self-awareness is profoundly shaped by who our family is, by where we come from, and by the work we do, among other factors. So when a person is raised in a dysfunctional family, is removed from his or her own culture, and has to work in a dead-end job, self-identity takes a triple hit. And when those three factors are severely distorted—when the dysfunction involves domestic abuse, the cultural transition is sudden, and the dead-end job is forced labor—well, such trauma could have lasting impact on the person and ripple effects into future generations.

Joseph could have checked "all of the above"—a background of abuse, social disadvantages, and hopeless situations—and resigned himself to an obscure, tedious life. Apparently he didn't.

He probably couldn't allow himself to. He was driven by a high calling and a firm belief that God was worthy of his obedience and loyalty, regardless of apparent setbacks. If anyone ever had a right to be eaten away by bitterness, Joseph certainly did. Most of his brothers wanted him dead. They settled for sending him away to a distant land in chains. Anything, as long as they didn't have to deal with him. And their venomous attitude toward him resulted in long, painful years as an outsider of extremely low means. How does someone highly favored by both his father and God end up as a falsely imprisoned slave? Where's the favor in that? It just didn't make sense.

We could ask the same questions. How do children of God, members of a royal priesthood who are seated with Christ in heavenly places, become victimized by unscrupulous people?

THE INFAMOUS COAT

The many-colored coat that Jacob gave Joseph has become the star of Sunday school lessons and Broadway musicals. But what exactly was it? No one knows for sure. The language is ambiguous—it can even be interpreted as a long-sleeve coat or an expensive garment of leisure rather than labor. (Some Egyptian paintings from about this time show prosperous Canaanites in long-sleeved, embroidered garments.) Scholars have put forth a number of speculations about Jacob's gift: that it was a robe of royalty, for example, or even that Jacob dressed Joseph in feminine clothing to remind him of Rachel, his favorite wife. Regardless of the specifics, we know for certain that the coat provoked intense jealousy and anger among Joseph's brothers. It made a major statement that Jacob intended to pass over his ten eldest sons and make Joseph his heir. In other words, in trying to do away with him, they weren't just getting rid of an annoyance. They were eliminating their biggest rival to their father's enormous estate.

We're promised mountain-moving faith and answers to all our prayers in Jesus's name. Yet we suffer, frequently at the hands of godless deeds. Far too often, the wicked seem to prosper and the righteous seem to miss out on the prosperity. The meek don't seem to be inheriting very much. Something is wrong with that picture.

But that's not how God sees things. He uses our worst predicaments to accomplish his purposes, both for our good and for the sake of his kingdom. He somehow factors human messiness into his best equations. And while he already sees the outcome of our story, we only see the obvious implications for the moment. And sometimes, as they did with Joseph, those implications appear devastating.

Pure or Proud? Genesis 37:2–11

Is Joseph an innocent and righteous son or an arrogant spoiled brat? A case can be made for either; the biblical text reports his behavior matter-of-factly without making any value statements on it. Consider the evidence:

- Verse 2: He reports his brothers' misbehavior to Jacob, but that doesn't settle the issue. If the behavior had been dangerous, blatantly sinful, or damaging to the family's business or reputation, it should have been reported. If not, it's petty tattling.
- Verse 4: His brothers hate him and can't bring themselves to speak kindly to him. The family's division of labor has him working not with sons of the "real" wives of Jacob (Leah and Rachel) but with the sons of the servants (Bilhah and Zilpah)—an arrangement likely enforced by the oldest of the brothers. Usually there are underlying reasons

13

SPICE TRADERS

Dothan served as a way station for travelers on a route between the northern Arabian Peninsula and North Africa, which explains why a band of traders happened to be passing by on the day of Joseph's captivity. These traders are alternately called Ishmaelites and Midianites in Genesis 37, most likely because those two groups were related and often intermingled. (Judg. 8:22–24 is another example that uses these names interchangeably.) This particular caravan was coming from Gilead, a region east of the Jordan River that was known for its balms and spices, and was loaded down with products to sell in Egypt. Because of the constant threat of bandits, wild animals, and extreme weather conditions, traders usually traveled in large groups—sometimes the donkeys that carried supplies and merchandise numbered in the hundreds—and were accompanied by armed guards. The traders bought Joseph for twenty shekels, a common price for slaves, equal to about two years' wages.

for such open animosity, but the text only tells us that Jacob loves Joseph more than the others and gives him an expensive robe. Does that alone stir them to jealousy? Or does Joseph provoke them by flaunting his father's favor?

- Verses 5 and 9: The brothers' hatred increases when Joseph informs them of his dreams. There are two likely reasons he would be foolish enough to do that on two separate occasions: (1) as suggested above, he is rudely flaunting his status in the family; or (2) he is naïvely trying to win his brothers' respect by saying, in essence, "God thinks I'm special too." Obviously, this has the opposite effect.

In favor of "innocent/righteous/naïve" is the fact that the Bible never speaks a negative word about Joseph. He's one of only a handful of others whose flaws are not directly mentioned. (Ruth, Esther, and Daniel—in addition to the most obvious case, Jesus—are most prominent among those select few.) The messianic symbolism in Joseph's experiences also supports the idea of his innocence, and the ensuing behavior of his brothers proves that they likely would have been bothered by a righteous son in their midst regardless of whether he flaunted it or not.

On the other hand, what does it say of the character of a seventeen-year-old that he tattles, displays his status symbol prominently, and blatantly defies social norms by expressing his visions of grandeur to older men in the family? After all, in a highly paternalistic culture in which fathers are the highest authority and sons are ranked by seniority, you don't just tell eleven men who are higher in the pecking order that they'll bow before you. And, in fact, Joseph's family may think he expects the dreams to have immediate implications—as in, "you should bow to me now."

JUST LIKE JESUS?

If Joseph's story has a familiar ring to it, consider another descendant of Jacob whose claims of future exaltation were considered arrogant. Jesus was sent to the other sons of Jacob (Israel) because of their Father's compassion, but his Jewish brothers plotted to seize him and kill him. He too was sold for pieces of silver, his coat was stripped from his back, he was cast into an empty grave that would not hold him for long, and then all Israel sat down to eat. (Jesus was crucified immediately before Jews celebrated the Passover meal.) And just as Joseph saved Egypt from famine, Jesus was sent to save Gentiles until the time of Israel's repentance, when, according to prophecy, the sons of Jacob will finally bow before him.

Regardless of the picture of Joseph you accept, the beginnings of his story are loaded with meaning and set the stage for what's to come.

Discuss

- Which image of Joseph speaks more profoundly to you: the Christ-like suffering servant or the young man who needs to be knocked down a couple of notches? Why?

  _____

  _____

- God's chosen people came from an extremely dysfunctional family. Is that encouraging to you or troubling? Why?

  _____

  _____

- Do you think it was God's will for Joseph to tell his family of his dreams, even if that meant coming across as arrogant?

  _____

  _____

Treachery: Genesis 37:12–28

Joseph's statements about himself come across as arrogant and boastful, whether they are intended that way or not, and his brothers' hatred nearly boils over. But the flocks need to graze far from home—a common occurrence in dry summers, when only the hill country still has vegetation—so the brothers leave Joseph at home and go to Shechem. (See Genesis 34 for details on the gruesome episode that had caused the family to move away from Shechem, where they once lived.) The breathing room between Joseph and his brothers is probably welcome to all, but it seems to last longer than expected. Considering the family's history in the hill country, Jacob has legitimate reasons for concern, so he sends Joseph to check on his brothers. When he gets to Shechem, he finds that they have moved on—perhaps the Shechemites' vivid memories flared up and forced them to leave—and tracks them down in Dothan, a town on an important trade route connecting Asia and Africa. And from their position in the hills, the brothers can easily see the teenager in the fancy robe approaching.

What happens next is shocking: an impromptu plot, a nearby dry well, and a brother betrayed by his own kin. Joseph finds himself stripped of his precious robe and stuck at the bottom of a cistern—a man-made hole in the local limestone, lined with plaster to hold water and, when dry, occasionally used for prisoners (see Jer. 38:6). Then these ten sit down to eat a meal while Joseph pleads for his life. Thanks to the entrepreneurial instincts of his brothers, his life is spared. He's drawn out of the well and sold to a caravan of Ishmaelites and Midianites on their way to Egypt.

Discuss

- Considering that Jacob loved Joseph more than his brothers, why do you think he sent him alone through a hostile region (Shechem) to men who were known to hate him and who had already demonstrated violent tendencies in chapter 34?

_____

_____

17

The Inconsolable Father: Genesis 37:29–36

Reuben, one of only two brothers to express concern for Joseph's life, returns to the cistern and finds it empty—much like Jesus's followers found an empty tomb centuries later. They dip his robe in goat's blood (which would later become symbolic of the Day of Atonement offering for sin) and show it to their father. When Jacob sees Joseph's "glory"—his expensive coat—he weeps for the sacrifice his beloved son made on behalf of his brothers as he sought for them. And as much as Jacob's duplicitous sons try to comfort him, they can't. Though a typical mourning period could last a week, a month, or seventy days, Jacob intends to mourn—to wear sackcloth and ashes—for the rest of his life.

Meanwhile, the band of Midianites turns a tidy profit when they arrive in Egypt, selling Joseph to a high-ranking official in Pharaoh's court. And though the Bible never describes his attitude, one can only imagine. He must have wondered why this turn of events is so radically contrary to those dreams he had.

Discuss

- Joseph had a very strong sense of his own future, and a well was probably the last thing he expected. If you had been in his predicament, how would you reconcile your situation with your belief in God's power and love?

_____

_____

_____

_____

_____

A Case Study

Imagine: Your father has been married four times, his ex-wives are still around (and obviously hate each other), you've had to move at least five times in your life, your grandfather on your mother's side is the slimiest salesman you've ever met, your uncle almost murdered your dad out of revenge long ago, your many siblings are split into opposing factions, one of your sisters was recently raped, two of your brothers once went on a killing spree, and your mom died giving birth to your little brother. Oh, and Daddy loves you best—and the others know it all too well.

- What obstacles would you have to overcome to "make something" of your life? What expectations do you think modern society would have for you?
- Would you see your upbringing as an asset in God's hands or a liability that limits your options? Why?
- In what ways might God be limited by the questionable influences in your life?

Rise and Fall, Round Two

GENESIS 39

In 1984, Darryl Hunt was convicted for murdering a local newspaper reporter in Winston-Salem, N.C. A hotel employee saw Hunt enter and then leave a bathroom in which bloody hand towels were discovered later that morning. Other witnesses had seen him near the murder scene. Though Hunt always denied his guilt, the jury had little trouble convicting him. He was sentenced to life in prison.

Ten years later, DNA testing cleared Hunt of sexual assault, which was an integral aspect of the murder case. Nine years after that, a man confessed raping and stabbing the reporter, and DNA results confirmed his confession. And that witness who saw Hunt at the hotel? And the others who saw him near the murder scene? Turns out they had misidentified Hunt, either

A MIXED VERDICT

Potiphar is called one of Pharaoh's "officials." The Hebrew word is *saris*, which literally means "eunuch," perhaps shedding some light on his wife's insatiable desire for Joseph. Specifically, he was "the captain of the guard," a title implying a high authority over the royal justice system. But in his fury after hearing his wife's story, he didn't sentence Joseph to the normal punishment for that crime: execution. Instead, he confined Joseph in a prison that operated under his own authority and apparently never said anything to undermine the warden's trust in the prisoner. It's possible he even commended Joseph to the jailer as a good steward. All of which has led commentators to wonder if perhaps Potiphar knew his wife well enough to see through her story but still felt pressure to take her word over that of a mere slave.

intentionally or by mistake. Hunt was released in 2004 after nineteen years behind bars.

Upon his release, Hunt offered his condolences to the mother of the victim and forgave everyone involved in sending him to prison and in keeping him there so long. Today Hunt leads a nonprofit advocacy group for wrongfully incarcerated people—who, surprisingly, number in the tens of thousands.

Injustice is hard to handle, and the temptation for the victim to nurse a grudge is almost irresistible. Though few of us will ever spend two decades in prison for a crime we didn't commit, we've all been misperceived, mistreated, or wrongly accused. We know what it's like to get the short end of the stick, to be victimized by someone who either didn't understand the situation or didn't care. And though we hardly realize it at the time, those are defining moments in our lives. How will we respond to unfairness? Will we get bitter, angry, or

CLOTHES TELL THE STORY

Similar to the way Joseph's dreams mark shifts in his life, his clothing dramatizes the way he's presented to others. The multi-colored coat was dipped in blood and presented to Jacob as evidence for Joseph's death. Potiphar's wife held the garment he left behind as evidence that he attacked her. Then, in a positive turn, he's later dressed in clothes that make him presentable in Pharaoh's court (41:14); and he's clothed in linen royal robes and presented to the Egyptian citizenry as a man of high authority. In fact, his clothing can be seen as a structure for his journey to the depths and then the heights. A royal robe marks his enslavement in Egypt, a servant's garment marks his imprisonment, typical Egyptian clothing marks his release, and a royal robe marks his exaltation. For some fascinating similarities, read John 13:3–12 and 19:2–5.

depressed? Or will we trust that we're safely in God's hands? We know the right answer to that question. But believing it is an entirely different matter. Few of us handle life's setbacks as Joseph did.

Favor: Genesis 39:1–6a

Joseph could have allowed himself to sink into depression and bitterness, but evidently he doesn't. Potiphar favors him, promotes him, and trusts him with his household. Those kinds of perks are given to those who are diligent and faithful, not to those who are defeated by adversity. If Joseph had had an issue with pride while living with his family, it was fading fast. It takes great humility to go from heir apparent in a wealthy family to servant in a foreign home, and Joseph does it with enough grace to earn the admiration of his master.

Discuss

- What attributes—think in terms of values, ethics, and attitudes—do you think Joseph must have displayed for Potiphar to favor him as he did?

_____

_____

_____

- Do you live your life in such a way that people see that "the Lord is with you"? What sorts of behavior might cause them to think that?

_____

_____

_____

Temptation: Genesis 39:6b–18

Potiphar's wife had taken a liking to Joseph, and she's pretty persistent in expressing it—"day after day," the text says. So Joseph doesn't simply have to endure a single seduction. He has to resist repeatedly and consistently.

Was Joseph really tempted by the proposition? The passage doesn't say, but rabbinic commentators from ages past have generally assumed that she was genuinely alluring. When verse 10 is chanted in synagogues, for example, the Hebrew word for "refused" is drawn out into a lengthy note, implying that Joseph may have really struggled with the possibilities. But speculation aside, he handled the situation with godly maturity. He avoided being with her, and when she cornered him, he ran. He may not have been able to foresee her false accusations, but he certainly knew that her displeasure wasn't to his advantage. Yet he chose harsh consequences over easy compromises.

In terms of God's purposes, this event is a major test of character for Joseph. It may have been advantageous for him to sleep with the boss's wife—the fast track into a position of power that might fulfill those dreams. But he demonstrates that integrity matters more to him than circumstances do. He thinks of his master's trust in him, and he thinks of God. This would be a sin against both of them. That isn't worth any amount of potential payoffs.

Discuss

- Which is harder for you: resisting a huge, one-time temptation or a lot of small, repeated temptations? Why?

  _____

  _____

  _____

  _____

- In what ways is Joseph's resistance against temptation a model for us? What temptation do you face that might require some of the attitudes he had and the steps he took?

  _____

  _____

  _____

  _____

Another Raw Deal: Genesis 39:19–23

Joseph has to be wondering why he has been getting such mixed messages from God. Dreams of exaltation, then a pit and slavery; steward of the household, then prisoner in a cell. And then the cycle seems to begin again. His stock starts rising, just as it had done in his family and in Potiphar's home.

When Joseph had been thrown into the well by his brothers, he pleaded for his life desperately (42:21). Now thrown into a cell, there's no hint of any protest on his part. Perhaps he has learned to suffer well and to trust God in the darkest circumstances.

Discuss

- How would you have responded if you were in Joseph's situation?

  _____

  _____

  _____

  _____

- First Peter 2:19–23 says that suffering unjustly and enduring it is commendable to God and, in fact, that followers of Jesus are called to suffer as He did. How did this idea play out in Joseph's life? How might it play out in your life today?

  _____

  _____

  _____

  _____

A Case Study

Imagine: God has called you to an extremely important task, and you've geared your life toward fulfilling that mission. But through a tragic turn of events, you find yourself languishing in prison for a crime you didn't commit. As far as you can tell, there's little hope for your release, and your calling now seems impossible. From all appearances, you've missed your destiny.

- How would you feel about the people responsible for your captivity? How would you feel about God?
- What would you say in your prayers?
- Which would seem larger to you: the power of your circumstances to defeat you or the power of God to deliver you? Why?

Contact with the Court

GENESIS 40

"I know we are the chosen people," Tevye said, looking heavenward. "But once in a while, can't you choose someone else?" That line from *Fiddler on the Roof* expresses the sentiment of quite a few Jews and anyone else who has ever experienced the hard blessings of God. Mary, for example, was "highly favored" enough to endure the stigma of unwed pregnancy and the brutal execution of her innocent son. From an eternal perspective, of course, being the mother of Jesus is an unimaginable glory. But the view from earth must have been difficult at times, just as it was with the martyrs, the prophets, David, Moses, and all

PALACE INTRIGUE

Why were the cupbearer and baker put in prison? No one knows for sure. It could have simply been that Pharaoh had been having indigestion more often than usual and wanted to send a message to his staff. Much more likely, however, is the possibility that a plot to poison the king had been uncovered. No such scheme could be carried out without the help of either the cook or the pre-taster, so both of them would have to be held until a full investigation could be launched and the conspirators had confessed which man was their inside help. The mention of an upcoming birthday feast for Pharaoh only serves to strengthen this theory, as such irregular, staff-heavy events provide a greater opportunity for treacherous plots to be carried out unnoticed. Regardless of speculation, however, a reasonable suspicion of guilt was apparently established. During the birthday feast, the cupbearer was exonerated, and the cook was publicly shamed and executed.

those leading back to Joseph. The cost of chosenness for all of them was extremely high.

Up to this point in Joseph's life, his entire family had seen the favor of his father, and Egyptians had seen the favor of his God. But what kind of favor? Potiphar recognized that God was with Joseph while knowing that he'd been sold as a slave. The head jailer saw that God was with Joseph while knowing that he'd been thrown into prison. They couldn't have seen an unknown God in the circumstances in which they first encountered Joseph, so they must have seen it in his more enduring characteristics. And even in the eyes of ancient Egyptians, it was obvious that divine favor and easy circumstances were not by any means synonymous.

That's true for us as well. We are divinely favored in Christ, blessed with the unimaginable glory of knowing him and sharing his inheritance. Yet life is sometimes mercilessly difficult. That wasn't a contradiction in Joseph's life, and it's not a contradiction in ours. If our difficulties were eternal and our blessings temporary, we wouldn't consider ourselves the subjects of God's favor. But for us, the situation is reversed. The trials are temporary, and the blessings are eternal. From the view above, our chosenness is a privilege.

After this session, Joseph's circumstances will take a dramatic turn for the better. His trials won't be over, but they will be far outweighed by his prosperity. Even as he sat in prison, he must have known that at some level because he continued to demonstrate faith and integrity. He still seemed to know he was blessed to be chosen.

THE DREAM THEME

Each major shift in Joseph's life is prompted by a pair of dreams—the two similar dreams that angered his brothers, the cupbearer's and baker's dreams that got him out of prison, and the pharaoh's dreams that elevated him to authority. In most of the ancient world, dreams were considered to contain revelations from deities or omens about what deities were planning to do. While many of them were filled with obscure symbolism and required skilled interpretation, Joseph's first two dreams had a painfully obvious meaning. The dreams of the cupbearer, the baker, and the pharaoh himself, however, were more cryptic. Most advanced cultures of this era, including Egypt, developed highly detailed manuals for dream interpretation. This literature was considered to be advanced knowledge, a sort of science curriculum for understanding the revelations of the gods. Joseph's revelation is clearly higher, as he explains Egyptian dreams without the aid of the culture's collective wisdom. His only source of interpretation is God.

Inside Information: Genesis 40:1–15

"Some time later . . ." the passage begins. A lot of time, in fact. Joseph was seventeen when he was sold by his brothers. Now he's in his late twenties, and he's a far cry from the promises of God—or at least what he understands of them. A decade is a long time to be spiritually "on hold." But God has already seen the end of Joseph's troubles, and the outcome isn't in doubt. His opportunities aren't hindered by long years or dark cells. Joseph's jail time may have seemed a lingering question mark to him, but from above, it's just one part of the bigger picture.

One of those opportunities is planted like a seed when two members of Pharaoh's court are imprisoned. Both the cupbearer and baker have significant rank and responsibilities. The cupbearer (wine steward/butler) is the quality-control supervisor for the king's food, testing it for poison at the risk of his life before setting it on the table. The person in this role might also function as a trusted adviser, as Nehemiah would later do for the king of Persia. And the baker has a high position too. Much more than a pastry chef, he is generally responsible for all food in the royal household and supervises everything that goes on in the kitchen.

The "captain of the guard"—presumably Potiphar, since this is the same title that introduces him in 39:1—puts these high-ranking officials under Joseph's supervision. One day Joseph notices more than the normal amount of stress on their faces and presses them for details. Seeing his concern, they begin to share the dreams that have disturbed them. The wine steward goes first, and Joseph blesses him with a very encouraging interpretation. Joseph also sees a window of opportunity; perhaps the cupbearer is his ticket out of prison.

Discuss

- What do you think Joseph thought about as he sat in prison for all of those years? What thoughts come to your mind when life doesn't work out as you expect it to?

  _____

  _____

  _____

  _____

- In 40:8, Joseph credits dream interpretation to God alone. Do you think this statement suggests that Joseph no longer trusts his own interpretations of his dreams? What does this statement say about Joseph's faith in God?

  _____

  _____

  _____

  _____

- What does it say about Joseph's character that the same man who had him thrown in jail has now entrusted him with two of the officers closest to Pharaoh himself?

  _____

  _____

  _____

  _____

Proof of the Prophet: Genesis 40:16–23

The way the text is worded implies that the chief baker hadn't planned to share his dream. Is he aware of his guilt and wary of a seer getting a glimpse of it? Perhaps. But when he hears the glowing interpretation of his colleague's dream, he decides to give

31

it a try. How he reacts upon hearing the bad news is unknown, but the next three days will seem like years. Is this Hebrew prisoner a prophet or a punch line? Only time will tell.

In three days, just as Joseph's interpretation said, the matter is settled. Pharaoh's birthday feast has been made more interesting with the climax of a palace drama. Both the wine steward and the baker are brought out of prison to attend the festivities. In this very public celebration, where nobility's attention is singularly focused, the verdict is rendered. The cupbearer is restored, and the baker is put to death—and, according to practices of the time, gruesomely hung on display as a warning to others. But Joseph's window of opportunity seems to close; he fades from the cupbearer's memory.

Discuss

- What would Joseph have missed if he had not taken an interest in the problems of his fellow prisoners? What does his friendship with them teach us about how God uses our relationships to accomplish his will?

  _____

  _____

  _____

- Why would God reveal the details of cryptic dreams to Joseph rather than simply giving the cupbearer a reminder to help Joseph out? What implications do you think both scenarios have for Joseph's ability to trust God?

  _____

  _____

  _____

A Case Study

Imagine: You've been stuck behind a desk in a dead-end job for years—not because you aren't qualified or ambitious but because no one has really noticed your qualifications or ambition. But one day you find yourself stuck in a broken elevator with one of your company's vice presidents, and he has nothing to do but talk with you. You tell him about your background and your dreams, and he tells you about what's going on in his personal life and in the upper echelons of the business. In fact, you're able to give him some insightful advice that will solve one of the company's ongoing crises, and he's truly grateful. It looks like the beginning of a very advantageous friendship. After several hours, you're rescued and say your goodbyes.

"Remember me next time you have an opening up there," you say to your new friend.

"I will," he answers. "I definitely will. Count on it." But he doesn't. Several openings come and go, and you never receive a call.

- What would you believe about God's involvement in your life during those years?
- How likely would you be to thank God for waiting and tell him you trust his timing? Looking back on it years from now, how likely do you think it is that you'd end up thanking him for the delay?
- Is it possible to get tomorrow's perspective into our minds today? If so, how?

When the Time Is Right

GENESIS 41

All of her life pointed to this one purpose. All of her dreams led her here. It had been in her heart as a child, and it only grew stronger since. She was destined by God to leave her friends and family behind and teach the gospel to this tribe.

But she had to do more than teach it. She had to live it. She was called to represent the light and truth of heaven in a very dark corner of the world, and she was determined to carry out her mission not as an outsider but as one of the tribe. She learned their language, developed their cultural habits, studied their beliefs, lived in their huts, ate their food, and wore their clothes—or what they considered "clothes." She became what they were in order to lead them into new life.

That's what incarnation is. That's how God came to us in Jesus and also how we are to go to others in his name. We may not be *of* the world, but we're certainly in it, and our purpose as believers while we're here is to live out the truth of God's kingdom in such a way as to impact the false kingdoms around us. In the words of Paul, "I have become all things to all men so that by all possible means I might save some" (1 Cor. 9:22).

This sort of incarnational ministry is essentially what God did with Joseph too. Joseph didn't choose it; it was imposed by the evil intent of his brothers and the sovereign will of God. But Joseph became "Egyptian" in all appearances in order to serve as God's preparation for times of need. Through his incarnation as a servant in a foreign land, God set him up to provide for a country, a region, and even his own brothers. Because much of his life was spent in sacrifice, many people were saved.

Crisis: Genesis 41:1–13

The cupbearer has served the royal table faithfully since that traumatic episode two years ago. Now another trauma is stirring up Pharaoh's household. Vivid dreams, obviously messages from the gods, have profoundly burdened the king. This is unusual; as

NUMBER TWO

In Canaan, Joseph rose to the second highest position in his family as his father's favorite son. In slavery, he rose to the second highest position in Potiphar's household. In prison, he rose to second in command under the warden. In the Egyptian hierarchy, he rose to second in command under Pharaoh. And after being reunited with his family, he again rose to second in position under his father. In every case, he was highly favored by the one highest authority—not unlike a man whose Father thundered from heaven: "This is my beloved Son in whom I am well pleased."

a divine being himself, his dreams are normally simple and clear. Not this time. He needs outside help. He calls in the scholars; they have experience in deciphering the activities of the gods. He summons the magicians' guild too, though their expertise is primarily medical. Frantically, Egypt's finest experts discuss the cryptic messages, but no consensus is formed. The national crisis is still a mystery.

The steward, however, remembers that awful time in prison, when the only hope he clung to was a dream explained to him by a Hebrew prisoner. And the Hebrew had been amazingly accurate; he foretold the outcome precisely. Maybe this man is the interpreter needed for such a time as this.

Discuss

- Because the pharaoh, supposedly a divine being, couldn't interpret his own dreams, calling for help might have been an embarrassment. With that in mind, why do you think he agreed to seek the advice of a Hebrew slave-turned-prisoner? What do you think would have been at stake for Joseph if he was wrong?

_____

_____

_____

Revelation: Genesis 41:14–36

Joseph's face is shaved and he's given clean, Egyptian clothes. That's a must for any honorable Egyptian of rank—and especially for anyone entering the presence of a deity like Pharaoh. And given a golden opportunity to claim divine favor, he declined. "I cannot do it," he said, pointing instead to a higher

LOADED NAMES

If Joseph had an internal struggle to understand his suffering, it was resolved by the time he had children. For one thing, he gave his sons Hebrew names—names from the land of his pain—even though he was thoroughly Egyptianized at this point. He named his first son Manasseh: "one who causes to forget." In other words, God's eventual blessing is great enough to make people forget the pain they went through to get to it. His second son is named Ephraim: "twice fruitful." God had made Joseph doubly fruitful in the land of his affliction—and the implication is that the affliction is a key ingredient to the fruitfulness. It's a repeated message in the Bible, with Job perhaps being the most recognizable parallel. After all of his inexplicable suffering, God blessed Job with exactly twice the amount of what he had in the beginning (Job 42:10).

God. Then with confidence and detail, he explains Pharaoh's dreams. Not only that, he advises the king on a very specific course of action. Only one response will save the nation from extreme hardship (and perhaps, by implication, save the throne for Pharaoh's dynasty): a rigorous savings program to preserve present wealth to reduce future poverty.

Discuss

- What difference in attitude do you see between Joseph sharing his dreams with his brothers years earlier and his deferring to God now in the presence of Pharaoh? What might have changed his attitude?

_____

_____

_____

- What kind of reception would Joseph's national savings program receive today in your country? Why?

_____

_____

_____

_____

Exaltation: Genesis 41:37–57

Joseph's descent into Egypt has seemed nearly endless. For thirteen years, the former "prince" of his household has suffered through the humbling stigmas of being a slave and a criminal yet without any recorded word of complaint. He has silently served. Now he is lifted up to a position of great honor. Pharaoh gives him a signet ring, representing the authority to issue decrees in the king's name; clothes him in royal robes of fine linen; gives him one of his own chariots; and presents to him a beautiful bride. "All the countries" come to him to be saved from this devastating famine.

The messianic theme of Joseph's life becomes even more apparent in his exaltation. Jesus suffered as a servant and a criminal, yet never protested. He was lifted up from the grave and ascended to heaven, where he was dressed in robes of righteousness. He sits at the throne of God, which is depicted in Scripture as the Lord's chariot, and bears the authority of the King's name. His father is arranging for him a beautiful bride, and all nations will come to him to be saved.

Discuss

- In what ways does the trajectory of Joseph's life match Jesus's incarnation as described in Philippians 2:5–11—an honored son, a humbled servant, then an exalted authority? In light of John 20:21—"As the Father has sent me, I am sending you"—how are Joseph and Jesus a model for us as we live as aliens in the world?

_____

_____

_____

_____

A CASE STUDY

Imagine: During a time of national prosperity, the president introduces a plan to increase taxes to "save for a rainy day." When pressed for reasons, it becomes clear that he puts a lot of stock in a prediction made by an immigrant who has an uncanny ability to predict recessions. The president fully acknowledges that the value of his plan probably won't be known until after he's left office. He just wants to leave a legacy of helping the public to be more disciplined in their spending for the national good.

- How do you think the public would react to the president? How do you think they would react if he were an authoritarian ruler?

- How would you personally feel about paying more taxes to help the country years from now?

- How disciplined are you—or *should* you be—in imposing spending restraints on yourself in order to (a) prepare for lean years or (b) give more generously to God's work?

Heart Check

GENESIS 42–43

Inspector Javert had a lot of faith in the law, and he was zealous about enforcing it. He envisioned a society in which honest people could live an ordered and respectable life and in which criminals—every last one of them—were safely behind bars. But in his zeal, he erred on the side of caution. Once a criminal, always a criminal, he believed. That meant that anyone who had a stained past was a threat to society. He was convinced that the human heart could not be changed.

Jean Valjean had a stained past, and once Javert discovered the true identity of this ex-convict, he was relentless in his judgments. It didn't matter that Valjean demonstrated remarkable mercy and generosity or that he consistently gave those around him every reason to trust his character. He had a criminal record, so he was a menace.

Javert realized at the end of *Les Misérables* that justice and mercy go hand in hand—that a person's heart can be changed by the mercy it receives and the time it takes to heal. The police inspector couldn't reconcile the demands of the law and the grace of God in Valjean's life, so he threw himself into the Seine River. His life had been spent on the quest to root evil out of society, and he finally discovered that evil could be rooted out of the heart. It was too much to handle.

Some people wear their offenses on their sleeves for the rest of their lives. They were betrayed or slighted in the past, and they never quite get over it. They let bitterness take over their life. Their zeal for vindication, for vengeance, or even for simple justice consumes them. They may say they believe in God's sovereignty, but they blame the people who hurt them

ONE-SIDED RECOGNITION

How was it that Joseph was able to recognize his brothers, but they weren't able to recognize him? When the brothers were last together, most of them were already adults, but Joseph was only seventeen. When they reunited, Joseph was nearly forty, shaven like an Egyptian, and dressed in Egyptian clothing and jewelry. He spoke the language of Egypt and continued to use an interpreter with his brothers, even though he could understand them. And as far as they were concerned, Joseph was a distant memory. He probably wasn't even alive. As for Joseph, it was easy enough for him to recognize them; they were ten Hebrew-speaking men who resembled the young adults he once knew, and hearing their names and observing their relational dynamics would have confirmed what had already become obvious to him. They were clearly his family. And he, in their eyes, was clearly an Egyptian through and through.

as if God had abandoned them in their circumstances. They are firm believers in the adage that "a leopard can't change its spots." And their lack of mercy does nothing to help them heal from their wounds. In fact, it only deepens them.

That could have been how Joseph's story turned out. He could have lived the rest of his days in bitterness or with an I-told-you-so feeling of superiority, seeking vengeance and assuming that his brothers were unreformable. But that's not how the story of God's people goes. It's hard to imagine God wanting to favor and vindicate Joseph if Joseph were only going to turn around and be unmerciful to his brothers. That's not a picture of grace any more than Javert's hyper-legalism was.

No, Joseph wasn't vengeful. His brothers returned, and he would pull for them to do the right thing. He would set them up to succeed, not to fail. He understood the character and the power of God. People *can* change. God can give them a new heart. His glory has the remarkable ability to grow in the soil of tragic, devastating events.

The Past Comes Back: Genesis 42:1–28

The famine is widespread—unusually so, since weather patterns normally create different conditions between Egypt and Palestine. But this famine is severe beyond Egypt's dominion, including Joseph's homeland. So Jacob sends his ten oldest sons to buy grain from the only country around that has some—keeping Benjamin at home, of course, because he's the last vestige of Jacob's love for Rachel. A tragic end to Benjamin would devastate the old man, and the last time his favorite son was alone with his brothers away from home . . . well, he couldn't take any chances of that happening again. Perhaps over

HOW MUCH DID REUBEN KNOW?

Reuben, the oldest of the brothers, tried to spare Joseph's life when his brothers threw him into a well and left him to die. He was going to secretly pull Joseph out later. But he wasn't there when the brothers changed their minds and sold Joseph to a caravan. When he returned to the empty well and saw that Joseph was missing, he was distraught. And the only evidence the Bible gives us of his knowledge of the situation is that he participated in dipping Joseph's coat in goat's blood and giving it to Jacob. Now, more than twenty years later, Reuben's assumption is still that Joseph is dead and that an accounting for his blood is required of them (42:22). Perhaps they all assumed that he was dead by now, but there's no clear indication that the younger brothers ever told him the truth about the caravan—which raises an interesting question. Did these dysfunctional siblings decide it would make more sense, math complexity notwithstanding, to divide Joseph's twenty-shekel selling price among nine people rather than ten?

the years, he has put some pieces of Joseph's mysterious demise together and would rather be safe than sorry.

The brothers arrive at the governor's headquarters and bow, and the governor remembers those long-ago dreams. But this isn't the fulfillment of them yet. There were eleven brothers and some parents in the dreams, and only ten brothers are here. He must figure out a plan to get his younger brother to come.

The plan seems perfect. Not only will it get Benjamin to Egypt, it will measure the heart of his brothers. The best test of repentance is to see how a person behaves when put in the same situation that led to his or her sin, so arranging an opportunity to betray the new favorite son will determine whether his brothers have changed. Joseph accuses them of spying (not an unusual charge leveled at foreign traders) and imprisons them for three days—perhaps some payback for his condition when he first arrived in Egypt. But why keep Simeon behind while the others leave to fetch Benjamin? It only makes sense that the second son of Leah should serve as a hostage for the second son of Rachel.

The brothers' predicament draws words of repentance out of them, but words are not enough. Not yet. And the trauma of finding silver in one brother's pack complicates matters even more. Far from a fortunate windfall, the unexplained money makes them instant fugitives. They'll never rest easy until they return it with apologies.

Discuss

- It had been more than twenty years since Joseph was separated from his family. Why do you think he made no effort to contact his family or even send servants to observe their situation—especially considering his vast resources and authority for the seven-plus years?

  _____

  _____

  _____

  _____

- Joseph's plan would effectively test his brothers' repentance, but how much of this experience do you think was a test of Joseph's ability to forgive?

  _____

  _____

  _____

  _____

The Dilemma: Genesis 42:29–38

Focus: Genesis 42:35–38

The burden of unexplained silver is worse than they thought. While telling their father of their Egypt experience, each of the brothers discovers that his pouch of silver that was paid for grain has been returned in his own sack. This large sum of money isn't likely to be overlooked in Egypt; they've probably already been identified as the culprits who tried to get away without paying. And what if Simeon has already been executed for the crime? If they show up in Egypt again, the consequences could be frightening for them too. And if they don't—well, Simeon is surely lost forever just as Joseph was. Jacob refuses to lose another. No, Benjamin cannot go.

Discuss

- Have you ever cried Jacob's lament in verse 36: "Everything is against me!"? How did God help you through it?

  _____

  _____

  _____

  _____

Back to Egypt: Genesis 43:1–25

Time passes. It's long enough for the family to deplete its stores of food and probably long enough for Simeon to wonder if he'll be in prison for life. But the famine persists, and so do the brothers. Jacob relents. He has little choice now. Benjamin must be allowed to go.

46

At least the brothers can return with extravagant gifts to smooth the way just in case that Egyptian governor holds a grudge over his missing silver. After all, Jacob knows a thing or two about buffering hostilities with gifts, as he tried to do with his brother Esau long ago. Choice imports from the east, some local specialties, and double the amount of silver ought to do it. And so the dreadful journey to Egypt begins.

Things don't go much better. The governor sees them and orders them to be taken to his house—a very bad sign. Will they become his slaves? They confess before finding out; perhaps he will have mercy. But they receive two surprises instead: assurance that they were accused of no wrong and a reunion with their brother Simeon.

Discuss

- What would you have done if, like Jacob, you were forced to choose between food for the family and risking the freedom—and possibly the life—of one of your sons?

  _____

  _____

  _____

The Dreamer's Vindication: Genesis 43:26–34

When Joseph returns, all eleven brothers bow down to him and offer him gifts. His first prophetic dream from more than two decades ago is fulfilled. Joseph again asks about "their" father, and they bow again—presumably this time in their father's name—and the second dream is fulfilled. Upon seeing Benjamin, his only full brother, he removes himself and weeps privately. And then, when he has returned, the brothers notice an astonishing phenomenon: they've been seated according to their birth order. How could the governor have known?

As for Joseph, is this an acknowledgment that birth order matters—a repentance of sorts for his insensitivity in telling his dreams years ago perhaps? Regardless, the family is together again in picture-perfect symbolism. The Egyptians and the brothers eat at two separate tables because foreigners are considered uncultured and vulgar; and Joseph sits at a third table—a man in between cultures, too high-ranking to eat with his own staff, and too Egyptian, as far as anyone knows, to eat with Hebrews. He's a symbol of what God has done. He bridges the gap between the needs of his family and the provision God has planned for them: a mediator between God and his chosen people.

This meal is decidedly different than the one his brothers ate as Joseph pleaded in the cistern. This one is sumptuous, and five times more so for Benjamin, who inexplicably receives the lavish favor of the governor. The brothers are in a perfect position to demonstrate the jealousy and hatred they once held for Rachel's offspring, but they don't. They've passed every test so far. There's only one more to go.

Discuss

- If Joseph had been bitter and resentful toward his brothers all of those years, do you think he would have received the same opportunities and developed the same leadership skills as he actually did? Why or why not? What effects does bitterness have on a person's emotional and social growth?

  _____

  _____

  _____

A Case Study

Imagine: You were only a teenager when a drunk driver slammed into your car one night, and you haven't walked since. That was twenty years ago, and all the hopes and dreams that filled you before the accident are a faint memory now, a shadow of what could have been. You've made something of a name for yourself now—you eventually realized you could accomplish a lot from a wheelchair—but your deepest passions never got off the ground. All these years later, you still remember his name and can't get his face out of your mind. He served time, of course; a few months in a minimum security facility. But you hope that deep in his soul he was punished longer than that. You hope he has often remembered what he did: how he stole your life from you and trampled on the dreams that once made your heart soar. And if you ever meet him again....

- Being as honest as you know how to be, how would you finish that sentence?
- In what ways do regrets and bitterness benefit the bearer of them? In what ways do they damage the bearer?
- How would you feel if you simply let go of past hurts and forgave whomever was responsible? Why is it so hard for us to do that?

An Open Door to a New Life

GENESIS 44–45

As a young man, George Müller dreamed of giving his life in mission work on foreign fields. He was rather impatient about it too, applying to mission societies before his friends and family thought he was ready. The mission societies also thought he wasn't ready and turned him down. Over time, his work in England grew into a vital orphanage that would eventually impact thousands of young lives. In operating the orphanage by faith alone, Müller saw miraculous provision of enormous sums of money—usually at the last minute. His life of faith continues to inspire Christians over a century after his death. Nevertheless, at the time, his dream of foreign missions seemed forever lost.

THE CUP OF DIVINATION

Divining chalices were common pieces of equipment for ancient authorities. Those skilled in divination would pour droplets of oil into a cup filled with water and interpret the movements of the oil for wisdom from the gods. But God emphatically prohibits any kind of divination, and even though his Law was given long after Joseph's death, the practice of divination would also have been contrary to God's nature during Joseph's life. So why did Joseph have a divining cup?

It may have simply been standard-issue for men in Joseph's position, and the text never says whether Joseph actually used his silver cup for such purposes. His steward tells Joseph's brothers that his master practices divination with it (44:5), but this could simply be an assumption about Joseph's remarkable ability to interpret dreams (and to seat "unknown" brothers by birth order) or an implied statement to the effect that "even if you steal my master's divining cup, you can't escape his gaze." Joseph essentially says the same thing in 44:15 when they return to him. His words have a threatening element, as if to say, "I know what you did twenty-two years ago." Regardless, the incident certainly made them feel that they were being closely watched.

At the age of seventy, however, God opened doors for Müller to travel extensively and teach the lessons he had learned to millions of people. Between 1875 and 1892, he took seventeen missionary tours through forty-two nations and preached thousands of times. Though the bulk of his life had been given to local ministry, God made up for "lost" time in the last years of his life. His dream, once thought to be a misguided desire of a youthful heart, was finally fulfilled.

Most of us have dreams that we abandoned long ago too. Some of them may have actually been misguided desires of youthful hearts, but some were probably placed in us by God himself. And when God places a dream in us, he intends to fulfill it. He may take years to do that sometimes, but he does not forget the seeds he's planted within us. No one can thwart his plans against his will.

We see that truth at work not only in Joseph's life but also in Jacob's. Joseph's vision of the future is fulfilled when his brothers bow down to him and he is able to offer them safety and provision out of his love for them. But Jacob's dream of passing down to his favorite son the promises once passed down to him has not yet been realized. At this point in the story, he doesn't know that God is going to reach down into his heart and resurrect his long-lost hope. As you read of his newfound joy, remember that God is still in the business of raising our lost hopes and fulfilling them in surprising ways.

The Ultimate Test: Genesis 44

Focus: Genesis 44:1–17; 30–34

Joseph's last test for his brothers involves putting Benjamin into a precarious situation, but one in which Joseph will have ultimate control. By having his silver cup hidden in Benjamin's sack, he sets his brothers up with a golden opportunity to allow Benjamin to be enslaved in Egypt, just as Joseph had been years before. Will his brothers betray Rachel's other son too—perhaps even suspect him of stealing the cup? Or will they demonstrate their repentance by sacrificing themselves for the sake of their father and their youngest brother?

Judah, the one who had long ago suggested selling Joseph rather than killing him, becomes the spokesman for the rest and defends Benjamin. He claims their innocence in this matter, but he does acknowledge their guilt in another. Their crime has followed them all these years, and now it has caught them. They

TWO MESSIAHS?

Hebrew Scripture is full of prophecies of the Messiah, but the varying predictions were hard for ancient rabbis to reconcile. In many prophecies, the Messiah is portrayed as a victorious king, a conquering warrior, and a mighty deliverer. In that respect, the Messiah is a Son of David. In other prophecies, however, the Messiah is a suffering servant, a humble authority figure who forgives and reconciles his people at great expense to himself. In that respect, the Messiah is a Son of Joseph. In an attempt to blend the two pictures, many rabbinic sages suggested that perhaps two Messiahs were coming to Israel, one from the tribe of Judah (*Mashiach ben David*, in Jewish literature), the other from one of the tribes of Joseph (*Mashiach ben Yosef*).

The tension is resolved in Jesus, of course, who came first as a humble, sacrificial servant who loved his brothers and longed to gather his people, and who will come again as a victorious King. There aren't two Messiahs, but there are two advents of the one Messiah; and each appearance has distinctive characteristics, thus fulfilling Scripture's prophecies. And, it should be noted, this Messiah was in fact born into the tribe of Judah—but also into the family of a carpenter named Joseph.

are all willing to suffer the penalty, he says. Even when Joseph insists that only Benjamin be punished, Judah offers himself in his brother's place. He demonstrates that he and his brothers are changed men.

Discuss

- Joseph gave his brothers an opportunity to demonstrate victory in circumstances similar to the ones that caused them to fail years before. Do you think God gives us similar tests/opportunities to reveal how we've learned from our past mistakes? If so, what are some examples of how he has done this in your life?

_____

_____

_____

_____

Full Disclosure: Genesis 45:1–15

Joseph can't last any longer. He breaks down emotionally and, through tears, reveals himself to his brothers in their own language. But they don't yet know of his forgiveness; all they have seen in their Egypt experience is the constant threat of prison or death. Now they think they realize what was going on—he was tormenting them. And they are "terrified."

But Joseph quickly assures them his intentions are good. "It was to save lives that God sent me ahead of you" (45:5), he said, emphasizing God's sovereign purposes behind all of the suffering that has occurred. This is a landmark statement indicating how God's sovereign plan takes into account our sinful actions. Once again, the messianic implications take center stage:

- His identity has been concealed from his brothers for years for him to minister to Egyptians, just as Jesus's identity had been hidden from his Jewish brothers while he ministered to Gentiles (Rom. 11:25).
- He weeps loudly for his brothers, just as Jesus wept over Jerusalem (Matt. 23:37).
- God's hand in painful circumstances is suddenly revealed when Joseph discloses his identity, just as God's plans in history will suddenly make sense when Jesus comes again (Rom. 11:26).

- Joseph declares that God sent him ahead to preserve a remnant on earth, just as Jesus preserves a remnant from among his brothers through their deliverance (Rom. 11:5).
- Joseph forgives his brothers, just as Jesus will forgive Israel's rejection of him (Jer. 50:20).
- Just as God worked out ancient Israel's salvation through the treachery of Joseph's brothers (Gen. 45:5), he works out the ultimate salvation of the human race through our treachery in killing the Messiah.

Discuss

- Whose plan was it for Joseph to go to Egypt—his brothers' or God's?

  _____
  _____
  _____
  _____

- Who or what killed Jesus: Jews and Romans (Acts 2:23) or God's own purposes (John 19:10–11)?

  _____
  _____
  _____
  _____

- Whose plan was being worked out when you made a bad decision or sinned greatly—yours or God's?

  _____
  _____
  _____

Immigration: Genesis 45:16–28

Pharaoh welcomes Joseph's brothers and invites the entire clan to move to Egypt, authorizing Joseph to give them whatever provisions they need. As Jacob had done for Joseph years before, and as Pharaoh had done for Joseph in Egypt, Joseph gives his brothers new clothes—Benjamin gets more than the others—to share his status and favor with them. He then sends gifts to his father and tells his brothers not to quarrel on the way. Is he expecting them to blame each other for their sin or to fight over their new blessings as they travel? This is the only time the word *ragaz* is translated as "quarrel" in Scripture; in every other occasion, it means "tremble" or "fear" or "be troubled." Perhaps Joseph knows that they may be overcome with emotion over what has happened or fearful that he is still planning some sort of revenge.

When they arrive in Canaan, Jacob finds their news hard to believe. So many questions must have arisen in his heart: Why have these sons not told him the truth all these years? Why hasn't Joseph tried to contact him? What happens now with all those promises of God that seemed to have been forgotten? Why would God send his people out of the land he promised them—and what will happen to the land if God's chosen family isn't in it? But in spite of the mystery of this turn of events, Jacob, who has been called by his old name to this point in the Joseph story, believes. His heart is revived. And he is called "Israel" once again.

Discuss

- Proverbs 13:12 says, "Hope deferred makes the heart sick, but a longing fulfilled is a tree of life." In what way does this verse describe Jacob's life? How have you experienced this truth in your life?

_____

_____

_____

_____

A CASE STUDY

Imagine: Years ago when you were young, you told a selfish lie that got you out of serious trouble but put a friend in prison. Your treachery has hounded you for twenty years; your future that once seemed so promising has been crippled by the weight of your conscience—along with God's displeasure, you're convinced— and life has spiraled downward. You've wrestled with depression and all kinds of habits that people develop to help them feel better, but those habits have made things worse. You can't even hold a job because of them. You would have told the truth at some point during your friend's lengthy imprisonment, but the revelation of your lie would have devastated the one person you love most and likely have landed you in prison for perjury. However you play it now, people's lives, including your own, are ruined.

One day, deep in debt and desperate for a job, you answer an employment ad and get called for an interview. Wearing your most positive, energetic face and the best clothes you have, neither of which is likely to impress anyone anyway, you go to your interview. When your name is called, you find yourself across the desk from your old friend—now out of prison and rapidly promoted to a position of influence. You barely recognize him because so much time and experience has passed. But he smiles as he recognizes you. He has probably looked forward to this moment for a very long time.

- How would you expect your friend to treat you? How would you respond if your friend told you that your back-stabbing had actually resulted in good things for him? Would you rejoice over God's sovereign purposes or continue to wonder "what might have been" if you hadn't done what you did? Why?

- If your friend hired you for the position, how comfortable would you be working for him? Would you be suspicious that any of his decisions affecting you might be twisted by deep-seated resentment?

- How would you answer these questions if God were the friend you once sinned against and you're desperately in need of him now? How readily do you accept grace?

The Still-Promised Land

GENESIS 46–47

"The government is forcing the bushmen to choose between starvation and leaving the land they have lived on for twenty thousand years." Those words come from the report of a human rights advocacy group responding to a Botswana policy forcing indigenous people out of the Kalahari game reserve. Though the locations and circumstances vary widely, the situation reflects a deep human concern: most people in the world feel very tied to the land they live on.

Ethnic nationalism has risen dramatically in the last half-century. Why? Because place and identity often go hand in hand. Headlines and international policy reports are full of concerns about refugees and "displaced people groups." Sometimes ethnic groups are scattered by war or economic hardship or political policy, and sometimes they simply fragment over time and lose their claim on a place. In any case, when people are separated from their territory, and especially when they are thrown into another culture, an identity crisis usually follows.

Forced immigration has been a pattern of Jewish history too. From Israel to other areas of the Middle East, North Africa, Western Europe, Eastern Europe, and then the Americas, Jews have frequently had to find a home in places other than their homeland. Psalm 137 lamented the fact long ago during the Babylonian exile: "How can we sing the songs of the Lord while in a foreign land?" But those who follow the Lord must learn to find their identity in him alone—even when the land of promise awaits.

Jacob and his family weren't exactly refugees. The only things compelling them to leave Canaan were a lack of food and an open door placed miraculously before them by God. But when a man, his father, and his father's father have all had dramatic divine encounters, received sacred promises, and built altars on very specific territory, leaving such holy ground can't be easy. It seems so contrary to God's plan, especially when the land was part of the plan to begin with.

Much like Abraham was asked to sacrifice Isaac—to give up the means of God's promise in order to demonstrate faith in the Promiser—Jacob was asked to leave the land where the promises would be fulfilled. It takes great faith to do that, and it's interesting that he got confirmation that he was doing the right thing after he was already on the way. Faith is often like that; it's validated only after the first nervous steps are taken. The people of God in any generation and in any area of life have to learn to walk by faith under those conditions. Wherever we are in life, we need to be able to hold firmly to a promise of God, even when the circumstances he allows dictate against the

SIBLING RIVALRY UNDONE

Genesis contains four major incidences of feuding brothers: Cain kills Abel, Ishmael and Isaac are destined to be at odds throughout history, Esau wants to kill Jacob after the blessing of the firstborn is stolen from him, and Joseph's brothers want him out of their life. The first incident leads to murder, the second leads to ongoing war, and the third leads to partial reconciliation but physical separation. Only the last story ends in full reconciliation. Significantly, this reunion is followed by the calling, blessing, prophecies, and growth of the twelve tribes of Israel. Unity lays the foundation for the work of God to be established.

promise. We need to go where he leads when it doesn't make sense—just like a man named Israel.

Reassurance: Genesis 46:1–27

Focus: Genesis 46:1–7; 26–28

His grandfather had planted a symbolic tamarisk tree there, and his father had built an altar on the same ground. It was the site of a sacred promise to establish Israel's family in the land of promise. Now as Jacob was passing by Beersheba, he stopped to offer sacrifices and worship—and God spoke again. Don't be afraid to walk in the opposite direction of this promise, God told Jacob. "I will surely bring you back again" (46:4). It's the eighth recorded time Jacob has heard his voice, and it will be the last.

Discuss

- How would you respond if God gave you a promise and then led you to walk away from it? Which would be

61

stronger—your questions or your trust? Can you think of any examples when God has done this in your life?

_____

_____

_____

_____

_____

Hope Fulfilled: Genesis 46:28–47:12

Focus: Genesis 46:28–34; 47:7–12

Jacob finally reunites with his beloved son Joseph. The reunion brings resolution and meaning to Jacob's life; he can now die in peace, knowing that the promises of God can and will be carried out through Joseph as well as his brothers.

Pharaoh may have welcomed the family to Egypt with open arms, but Egyptians in general have little regard for the nomadic shepherds who often settle in the northeast delta region—much in the same way most immigrant populations today are marginalized by a dominant group. In this case, however, it pays to be ostracized. Israel can keep its distinctive identity by avoiding integration with Egyptian society, as well as having plenty of fertile land for their livestock to graze.

When Jacob is introduced to Pharaoh, the patriarch blesses the king. That's more than a nice sentiment; it's a picture of which man ranks higher in God's eyes. (Hebrews 7:7 says that the lesser person is blessed by the greater.) The covenant God made with Abraham, Isaac, and Jacob includes a promise to bless the nations through them. In blessing Pharaoh, Jacob is keeping the covenant and professing his faith in God's promise.

INDENTURED SLAVERY

The practice of selling oneself to servitude, as in 47:21–25, was common in ancient civilizations. The term of one's slavery could be very short—even just a day—or it could be for months, years, or even for life. In God's law later given to Moses, this kind of servitude was limited among Hebrews to six years (Exod. 21:2), after which a Hebrew slave must be set free. Foreign slaves in Israel, however, could be kept permanently. Under Joseph's economic policy, Egyptians gave their land and their labor to the kingdom, which in turn rented it back to them for twenty percent of their production. The other eighty percent was theirs to use as they saw fit. Ironically, Jacob's descendants ended up as slaves of the Egyptian government—apparently much more tightly controlled than slaves in Joseph's arrangement—which led to the events of Exodus.

Discuss

- In what ways has God fulfilled his promise to bless the nations through ancient Israel? What role do Christians have in blessing the nations today?

  _____
  _____
  _____
  _____

A Place of Rest: Genesis 47:13–31

Joseph's economic plan has greater implications than simply feeding Egypt and its surrounding nations during a famine. It becomes the occasion to cultivate greater loyalty toward Pharaoh in the hearts of his people. It also serves to make Pharaoh the greatest landowner in the region. People begin selling their land to the government in order to buy food—and they are glad to do it, considering the unappealing alternative of starving to death. Pharaoh leases the land back to those who once owned it; they are obligated only to give him twenty percent of their produce.

As Jacob approaches the time of his death, he presses Joseph to take an oath. He wants a solemn pledge that his remains will eventually be buried in the family's tomb in the Promised Land.

Discuss

- Why do you think it mattered to Jacob to have his bones transferred from Egypt to the family tomb in Canaan? What does Joseph's oath demonstrate about his faith?

_____

_____

_____

_____

_____

_____

A Case Study

Imagine: You're a recent immigrant to the United States, and it isn't easy. You don't understand English very well yet, you don't have enough money for transportation or a decent roof over your head, your kids aren't getting much to eat, and, on top of that, natural-born citizens seem to resent the fact that you came. But even if you had known about all the difficulties, you still would have chosen to come. Your home country is ravaged by war and poverty, and life there was extremely difficult. Your choice was really quite simple: remain at home and let your family live in constant danger of violence and hunger; or move to the U.S., listen to the complaints about your presence, and hope that your children have a better chance in life. You'll endure an awful lot for that hope.

- To what degree do you think you would want to integrate into the dominant culture? What obstacles might hinder you from doing that?
- What would you say to people who think you should go back to your own country?
- In what ways does this situation illustrate the spiritual truths of living as aliens and strangers in the world (1 Pet. 2:11)? How do we retain our distinctive identity as Christians while also integrating into and blessing the society around us?

Legacy

GENESIS 48–50

Three generations had gathered for the Sabbath, and the house was full of noise. But when it came time to light the candles, the grandfather quieted everyone for the blessing. He went around to each of his sons and daughters and grandchildren to place his hands on their heads and speak words of blessing over them. "May God make you like Ephraim and Manasseh," he said to the boys. To the girls, he said, "May God make you like Rebekah and Sarah." Among these formal words of blessing, he also anticipated their future. His knowledge of each one's personality and his desires for their welfare blended into a verbal portrayal of their potential as God's children. His blessing was one of the most profound aspects of the legacy he would leave them.

This scene plays out in the homes of Torah-observant Jews on the eve of Sabbaths throughout the year. It is an act of obedience to the words of Genesis 48:20 and a continuation of the practice of Genesis 49, which describes the legacy Jacob wanted to leave to his children and his children's children. He wanted the promises of God not to be forgotten in future generations.

We all want to leave a legacy. We want the resources we've gathered and earned over the course of our lives to be invested in meaningful ways, so we give inheritances to our children and endowments to organizations whose work we believe in. We want our name to live beyond our own life span, so we try to preserve our accomplishments in tangible formats. We want everything we've worked for in this life to impact the lives of others after we're gone. The desire to leave a legacy seems to be embedded in our soul by our Creator.

What kind of legacy? That depends on each person's convictions and passions, but it's a worthwhile question to ask ourselves at any point in our life. If we were frequently to ask ourselves, "What am I doing in this stage of my life that will last beyond my years?" a lot of priorities would fall in place. And as children of God, we can look to make an impact beyond human history.

A DOUBLE BLESSING

At the beginning of Joseph's story, Jacob designated Joseph as his heir by endowing him with a foretaste of wealth: an extravagant coat. That meant, according to Hebrew tradition (and law, after Moses), that he would receive a double share of his father's estate. Now at the end of the story, Jacob makes good on that pledge. He adopts Joseph's two sons as his own, giving them each one share of the estate. Through his sons, Joseph's piece of the inheritance is, as planned, a double portion.

The time, money, talents, skills, and relationships we have today can be leveraged for eternity. We have the unique privilege of turning temporal resources into everlasting gain.

The last three chapters of Genesis are largely about the legacy left by the patriarchs. From their offspring will come an entire nation of chosen people who will be silent for the next four hundred years. But when we read of them again, it will be an epic to remember forever. God will establish this nation by giving them his law and establishing them in a Promised Land. Through them, the kingdom of God will be cultivated to bear fruit forever.

The Blessing: Genesis 48

Jacob, weathered enough for Pharaoh to have remarked about his age, falls ill, and Joseph is summoned with his two sons.

JOSEPH'S BONES

Joseph died at 110—the age Egyptians considered the perfect length of a divinely blessed life—and his body was handled in the typical Egyptian way: mummification. Before he died, he made his family swear to bury him in the land of promise, which Hebrews 11:22 commends as an exemplary act of faith. As it turns out, his embalming was providential. It would be four hundred years before Israel left Egypt. But when they did, Joseph's wish was not forgotten; Moses took his remains out of Egypt when the Hebrews fled (Exod. 13:19). Israel carried them for forty years in the wilderness and buried them on Jacob's tract of land at Shechem (Josh. 24:32). Symbolically, just as Joseph's body could not be held in the land of Israel's captivity, Jesus's body could not be held in the place of our captivity—this world and the grave.

Jacob effectually adopts Ephraim and Manasseh to be "just as Reuben and Simeon" are to him. In other words, he gives his two grandchildren through Joseph first and second rank among his own sons, a major rearrangement of the family inheritance. In circumstances reminiscent of the blessing Jacob received from his father, Isaac—an old man who couldn't see well and mistakenly blessed the younger son first—Jacob puts his right hand on the younger (Ephraim) and his left on the older (Manasseh). Certain that Jacob can't see straight, Joseph tries to correct him. But this time the subversion of birth order isn't by deception or mistake. Ephraim and Manasseh are blessed and, like Gentiles centuries later, grafted into the nation of Israel; and Joseph is assured that the family will one day return to the land of promise.

Discuss

- Why do you think Jacob insisted on switching the birth rank of Ephraim and Manasseh?

  _____

  _____

  _____

- On a larger scale, why do you think the early history of God's people is filled with so many instances of subverted birth order (Isaac over Ishmael, Jacob over Esau, Joseph over his brothers, and Ephraim over Manasseh)—even though the patriarchal culture heavily emphasized the status of the firstborn son?

  _____

  _____

  _____

  _____

The Future: Genesis 49

Focus: Genesis 49:1, 8–10, 22–26, 29–33

Chapter 49 functions as a charter document for the tribes of Israel. Jacob blesses each of his twelve sons with descriptions of their character and prophecies of their future. The blessings for Judah and Joseph are noteworthy—Judah for the messianic prophecies foreshadowing Jesus, who would be born in the tribe of Judah; and Joseph for the favor bestowed on him by a father who had long thought he would never have this privilege. After instructing his sons to bury him in the family burial cave, Jacob breathes his last.

Discuss

- Why do you think blessings were taken so seriously in Scripture? How important do you think formal blessings are in Christian families today? Why?

  _____

  _____

  _____

  _____

  _____

The End of the Patriarchs: Genesis 50

Jacob's death is observed in thoroughly Egyptian ways—a forty-day mummification, a seventy-day period of mourning (professional mourners were often hired for such occasions), and a sarcophagus.

Joseph asks Pharaoh's permission to go with the family to Canaan to bury their father, promising to return. Why the pledge? Perhaps the thought of staying in the Promised Land is tempting. After all, the famine is likely over at this point, and God had promised a return. Other than the prediction of four hundred years in a foreign country, what would keep the family of Israel in Egypt? But Joseph has responsibilities, and his family is settled in a fertile land. The time is not right. Nevertheless, Israel's deliverance is foreshadowed by the event. The route taken back to Canaan is odd and indirect, but it matches the path God will lead Moses and Joshua to take centuries later. Jacob's burial is a small picture of the Exodus.

After Jacob's death, Joseph's brothers wonder if he has simply shown restraint for his father's sake. Will he retaliate for their treachery now? Joseph assures them he will not and reiterates the principle of 45:5. But this time he states it even more strongly: "You intended to harm me, but God intended it for good to accomplish what is now being done, the saving of many lives" (50:20). It's one of the greatest statements in Scripture, revisited by Paul in Romans 8:28. And with a life filled with peace and prosperity for the rest of his days, Joseph lives to the blessed age of 110, knowing that his descendants have a special calling and a promising future.

Discuss

- In light of 50:20, is it possible for a faithful believer to miss God's purpose for his or her life?

  _____

  _____

  _____

  _____

  _____

- Psalm 139:16 says that all the days ordained for us were written in God's book before they came to be. How does this verse apply to Joseph's life? How does it apply to yours? In what ways is it comforting to you?

  _____

  _____

  _____

  _____

  _____

  _____

A Case Study

Imagine: For as long as you can remember, you've been told daily that God has chosen your family for special purposes and that your divine mission in life is to honor the family name, build up the family business, and pass the family identity down to the children you'll have one day. There are certain privileges bound up in this calling—knowing that God will favor you, for one—but there are some pretty heavy responsibilities too. Sometimes the weight of those responsibilities has nearly crushed you, and you've felt trapped. That's why you separated yourself from your extended family last year and don't even want the marriage or career they expect of you. But in spite of your new life, there are things about the old life that you miss. And deep down, you have a certain confidence that God will fulfill your destiny in spite of—or perhaps through—the different path you've taken.

- How do you feel about God's calling being your true identity? Which does your mind tend to focus on more: the privileges or the responsibilities of your calling?
- By walking away from a group-defined purpose (whether of a family, a church, or anything else), in what ways might you miss God's plan? Do you think it's possible for your "rebellion" to end up being part of God's plan—or at least how he works out his plan for you?
- In what ways have you seen God use your past mistakes to work out his purposes in your life?

Conclusion

A more fruitful life for the kingdom of God has rarely been lived. Joseph's was a life of remarkable integrity, honor, faithfulness, stewardship, and humility. And look at the fruit of such a life: through Joseph, God preserved the race through whom he would send his Son to save humanity from its rebellion. What began in the tumultuous lives of Jacob's twelve sons led to a chosen nation, a miracle-filled history, a royal priesthood, an eternal inheritance, and the blessing and favor of God on all who love him. No wonder Joseph is seen as a picture of Jesus, a foreshadowing of the ultimate Savior. He represented the character and the mercy of God among the nations of the world—and even among his own brothers.

Leader's Notes

Session 1

Genesis 37:12–28. So the group won't have to spend time reviewing the story of Genesis 34, you may want to read that chapter ahead of time and briefly summarize it during the session. The influence of this story of Dinah's rape and Simeon and Levi's revenge is subtle but definite in chapter 37. It highlights family dynamics and explains the potential danger the brothers faced as they shepherded in the Shechem area.

Genesis 37:31. The way Revelation 19:13 symbolizes Jesus's sacrifice is highly reminiscent of Joseph: "He is dressed in a robe dipped in blood."

A Case Study. How does this scenario parallel Joseph's early life?

- "You've had to move at least five times in your life": Genesis 30:36; 31:17–18; 33:18; 35:1.
- "Your grandfather on your mother's side is the slimiest salesman you've ever met": Laban had a long history of deceiving Jacob, promising Rachel in marriage but secretly giving him Leah first, and then engaging in questionable ethics in using Jacob's labor and sharing the family business with him.
- "Your uncle almost murdered your dad out of revenge long ago": Genesis 27:41 describes Esau's attitude toward Jacob upon having his father's blessing stolen; and Jacob was fully prepared to encounter the same attitude upon their reunion years later (Gen. 32:6–11).
- "Your many siblings are split into opposing factions": as discussed in the introduction and the commentary in this session.
- "One of your sisters was recently raped": Genesis 34.
- "Two of your brothers once went on a killing spree": Simeon and Levi's response to the rape of Dinah (Gen. 34).
- "Your mom died giving birth to your little brother": Genesis 35:18.

The last question in the case study discussion should ultimately end with an encouraging answer: "He isn't." Take this opportunity to remind participants that no one's background is an obstacle to God's purposes. Ever.

Session 2

Genesis 39:1–6a. If you have time during the discussion of this section, consider reading Ephesians 6:5–8 and/or Colossians 3:22–24. Paul's words of wisdom to slaves were modeled by Joseph centuries before they were written.

Session 3

Genesis 40:1–15, second discussion question. The set of questions on Genesis 40:8 are intended to stir a discussion about how much Joseph might have understood about the dreams he had shared with his brothers. Saying that interpretations belong to God could have meant: "Now I fully understand the implications of my dreams because God has revealed his interpretation to me." Or it could have meant: "Only God knows what my dreams meant because I sure can't tell anymore." Or, of course, Joseph might not have been thinking of his own dreams at all. The real issue worth discussing here, however, is how group members might feel about their life's trajectory seeming to go contrary to what they felt in the past to be their calling or the promises God had given them. Undoubtedly, this will be relevant to the experiences of some participants, if not all.

Session 4

Genesis 41:50. If you have time to include an interesting footnote, you may want to describe a first-century piece of "historical fiction" about Joseph and his wife, Asenath. Scholars believe *Joseph and Asenath* was written by a Jew, not a Christian, about the time the gospels were being written. The story tells of Asenath's pagan beliefs, a divine encounter with a "Son of Man" figure who looked exactly like Joseph, her abandonment of Egyptian religion in favor of Joseph's God, and her marriage to Joseph. The writer portrays Joseph as a Messiah figure and Asenath as the prototype of Gentile/pagan converts to Judaism—using symbolism of eating "bread of life," drinking from the "cup of immortality," and coming together in a divine bridegroom/bride relationship. It's an embellishment of an Old Testament story in dramatic—and, according to most scholars, unintentional—Christian symbolism.

A Case Study. This case study may lend itself particularly well to a political-style debate among policy experts or news commentators. Consider letting participants role-play the situation. Regardless of your format for this discussion, eventually steer participants toward some of the personal implications. The purpose of this scenario is not only to understand Pharaoh's situation more clearly but also to stress the importance of financial solvency on both national and individual levels. If this leads into a discussion of wise Christian stewardship of God's resources, all the better.

Session 6

Genesis 45:1–15. The discussion questions in this section should provoke some tension between human sins and mistakes and God's sovereign purposes, as the harmony between these two forces remains a mystery. The Bible affirms the truth of Romans 8:28 but never explains in detail how God does this. Ultimately, the discussion should lead participants to realize that each of these three discussion questions has a both/and answer rather than an either/or answer.

Session 8

A Case Study. This scenario brings several elements of the Joseph story into play: the sovereignty of God in grafting human flaws and frailties into his overall purposes; ability (or inability) of chosen people to truly diverge from their destiny; and Jewish identity and the prophetic history of the twelve tribes. On this latter point, your group will likely have at least one member who has felt pressured by family expectations and identity issues. While families today can't necessarily claim divine edict to back up their calling as Jacob's family could, the tension between group purposes and individual desires is the same. Discussing the dynamics involved in this tension will help shed light on what it means to be in the family of God.

Bibliography

Alexander, David, and Pat Alexander. *Zondervan Handbook to the Bible*. Grand Rapids: Zondervan, 1999.

Berlin, Adele, Marc Zvi Brettler, and Michael Fishbane, eds. *The Jewish Study Bible*. Oxford and New York: Oxford University Press, 2004.

Chilton, Bruce, et al. *The Cambridge Companion to the Bible*. Cambridge and New York: Cambridge University Press, 1997.

First Fruits of Zion. *Torah Club*. Volume 2: *Shadows of the Messiah*. Marshfield, MO: First Fruits of Zion, 1994–2004.

Hoerth, Alfred J. *Archaeology and the Old Testament*. Grand Rapids: Baker Books, 1998.

Morris, Henry M. *The Genesis Record: A Scientific and Devotional Commentary on the Book of Beginnings*. Grand Rapids: Baker Books, 1976.

Pink, Arthur. *Gleanings in Genesis*. Chicago: Moody, 1922.

Shanks, Herschel, ed. *Ancient Israel: From Abraham to the Roman Destruction of the Temple*. Upper Saddle River, NJ: Prentice Hall, 1999.

Snell, Daniel C. *Life in the Ancient Near East*. New Haven: Yale University Press, 1997.

Telushkin, Joseph. *Biblical Literacy: The Most Important People, Events, and Ideas of the Hebrew Bible*. New York: William Morrow, 1997.

Walton, John H., Victor H. Matthews, and Mark W. Chavalas. *The IVP Bible Background Commentary: Old Testament*. Downers Grove, IL: InterVarsity Press, 2000.

**WALK
THRU THE
BIBLE**®

Helping people everywhere
live God's Word

For more than three decades, Walk Thru the Bible has created discipleship materials and cultivated leadership networks that together are reaching millions of people through live seminars, print publications, audiovisual curricula, and the Internet. Known for innovative methods and high-quality resources, we serve the whole body of Christ across denominational, cultural, and national lines. Through our strong and cooperative international partnerships, we are strategically positioned to address the church's greatest need: developing mature, committed, and spiritually reproducing believers.

Walk Thru the Bible communicates the truths of God's Word in a way that makes the Bible readily accessible to anyone. We are committed to developing user-friendly resources that are Bible centered, of excellent quality, life changing for individuals, and catalytic for churches, ministries, and movements; and we are committed to maintaining our global reach through strategic partnerships while adhering to the highest levels of integrity in all we do.

Walk Thru the Bible partners with the local church worldwide to fulfill its mission, helping people "walk thru" the Bible with greater clarity and understanding. Live seminars and small group curricula are taught in over 45 languages by more than 80,000 people in more than 70 countries, and more than 100 million devotionals have been packaged into daily magazines, books, and other publications that reach over five million people each year.

Walk Thru the Bible
4201 North Peachtree Road
Atlanta, GA 30341-1207
770-458-9300
www.walkthru.org

Read the entire Bible in one year, thanks to the systematic reading plan in the best-selling **Daily Walk** devotional.

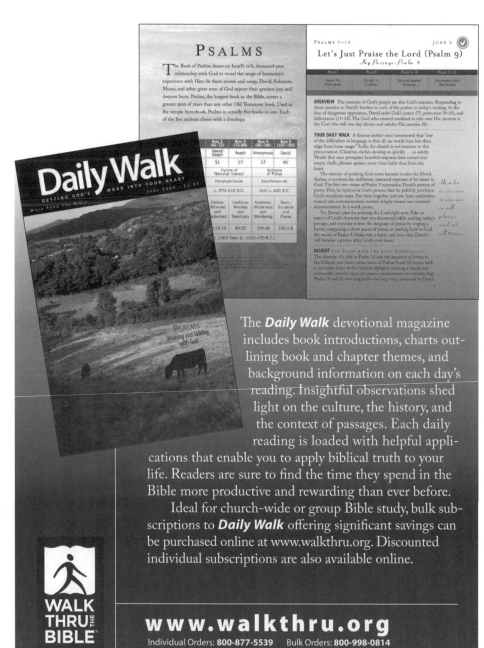

The **Daily Walk** devotional magazine includes book introductions, charts outlining book and chapter themes, and background information on each day's reading. Insightful observations shed light on the culture, the history, and the context of passages. Each daily reading is loaded with helpful applications that enable you to apply biblical truth to your life. Readers are sure to find the time they spend in the Bible more productive and rewarding than ever before.

Ideal for church-wide or group Bible study, bulk subscriptions to **Daily Walk** offering significant savings can be purchased online at www.walkthru.org. Discounted individual subscriptions are also available online.

WALK THRU THE BIBLE

www.walkthru.org